MANHASSET STORIES:
A Baby Boomer Looks Back

Suzanne McLain Rosenwasser

Manhasset Times
Media Group, LLC
2011

MANHASSET STORIES
© 2011 Suzanne McLain Rosenwasser.
All rights reserved.

Printed in the United States of America.

For further information, address:
Manhasset Times Media Group, LLC,
visit
www.suzannerosenwasser.com
or chat at
http://www.facebook.com/manhassetstories

ISBN:978-0-615-52311-8

Library of Congress (PCN): 2011916326

Cover Art: Michael A. Rosenwasser
Author Photo: Christopher McLain
Proofreader: MTMG and Mia Kishel

TO MY PARENTS:

Edie O'Neill McLain

and

James Murphy McLain Sr.

who gave me Manhasset with love

TABLE OF CONTENTS:

PREFACE
Looking Back with Manhasset Baby Boomers

We lived a privileged childhood growing up when we did in Manhasset and I think the greatest of those privileges, beyond the material ones, was the freedom we enjoyed in that world.

I sat with a group of Georgians recently who had read JR Moehringer's THE TENDER BAR. They asked me to speak when they learned of my roots in Manhasset. Mostly they wanted to know:

"What makes it such a special place? What is it about Manhasset that compels, first the writer and then the reader, to react so lovingly?"

My guess is - and I can only talk about the three decades following the 50s - a generation of Baby Boomers grew up with the town as it was growing up itself.

For us the magic of Manhasset has to do with timing, when all was new.

It was a new middle class. The families were young and new. The suburbs were a new concept. The highways to Long Island were new. The shopping centers and area parks were new.

I'm sure there were similar neighborhoods all over Long Island which were also electrified with the common bond of home ownership. In fact my husband grew up in a Levitt enterprise in Hicksville.

He and I have talked about the Manhasset phenomenon and he's witnessed it in our 40 years together. He does not claim to have had a like experience during the same time on the same Island, and neither do others with whom we've chatted.

So here's my theory about the magnificence of Baby Boomer Manhasset:

We lived in houses that skirted the estates of Gold Coast wealth with the most important city in the world just a brief train ride away. The new residents of Manhasset had the fire of post WWII in their bellies, Fifth Avenue stores at their fingertips, and an economy that was growing in leaps and bounds.

A change in perspective had to occur on Long Island's North Shore after the Great Depression conquered and divided the holdings of former land barons.

By the 50s, the generations born to the remnants of those manors had merged with the emigres of the New York boroughs - first and second generations of European immigrants - providing the emergence of an array of cultures. Our ethnicity was still so much a part of who we were then.

We lived in an epicenter of the changing times.

Jim Brown made lacrosse and football history at Manhasset High School in the early 50s and in '55, Temple Judea began to lay a solid foundation for Jewish families on Searingtown

Road. My St. Mary's High Class of 1965 included one student of color and, not long after graduation, some brave kids began to recognize their rights to choose whom to love.

Growing up I had friends whose homes included thoroughbred horses and friends who had nothing more to offer than a great spirit of adventure.

I played with a girl whose father had been a German wrestler. They had mats in their basement and a huge painting of her dad in a pugilistic pose hanging on the wall, with billets in German announcing his matches around it.

One friend's British mother served us tea from a thermos when we ice-skated at Copley Pond, and a dear friend's father, a doctor of Italian descent, hung a huge piece of roped hard-cheese (to age) in the shower off the kitchen of his five bedroom, Strathmore Vanderbilt home.

Johnny Desmond, a major television star of "Your Hit Parade," was a Strathmore neighbor and we played with his girls. He liked to take us for rides in his Jaguar convertible, even I knew that was cool.

Then just a few blocks away, I partook in some awesome slumber parties at Our Lady of Grace when it was just a convent. An incredibly exciting, new friend had arrived at St. Mary's from Queens. Her parents were to be the caretakers of the old estate. What can I say? The opportunities, while guests on the vast grounds of sleeping nuns, were endless. I won't name you, but there are people reading this now who went skinny dipping in the good sisters' pool. You know who you are.

Everything that became really large after the 60s was so much smaller then. But that's not to say the stress of living such a perfect life came without a costly toll.

Our neighbor killed himself with a rifle early one morning. I can still hear the sound of the shot and I was only 9.

During my eighth grade year at St. Mary's, four of the students in my class lost a parent.

I was one. My father died of a massive coronary while at a business lunch in Manhattan.

The other three deaths were equally as sudden, and a score more of our parents died before we graduated from college.

Our neighbors were killed tragically in accidents and incidents through the years, and before we knew it, we were losing Manhasset sons in Vietnam.

And alas, alcohol - the spirit that was everywhere we went - became Manhasset's Stealth Bomber. It took some of our friends, destroyed some of our families, and scared some of us straight if we were lucky.

Perhaps this is one other reason for the uncommon bond of Manhasset Baby Boomers:

We shared a golden era, but it didn't spare us from steely pain.

We had to grow up and, you know as well as I do, once you commit yourself to adulthood, it's a long time before you get to look back.

So I've chosen to dwell on the times we enjoy remembering.

Throughout my 60 years I've felt these moments of Manhasset in my bones, as have the friends who've stood at my side since we first smiled at each other.

When I began to publish feature stories about Manhasset in 1991, I learned about the many Manhasset Boomers who share that feeling.

Then I found a Facebook page called "I Grew Up in Manhasset..." and every question I ever had about whether the love I feel for my hometown is universal was answered.

We form a multitude.

Welcome home,

Suzanne McLain Rosenwasser,
November, 2011

Seeking Old Manhasset
in the Shadows of Memory

My family moved to Manhasset the same year as Lord & Taylor, Best & Company and W.J. Sloan's did. It was 1951, the year Manhasset's Miracle Mile was advertised as a "new idea in shopping."

I considered it a small town, but there were 15,000 books in the Manhasset Public Library then, one for each resident. Captain Video (Al Hodge) lived there and so did radio hosts, Tex and Jinx Falkenberg. Johnny Desmond of "Your Hit Parade" was soon to come.

Peck & Peck, the Onderdonks, the Paysons, the Paines, and the Whitneys had been there for decades, and the Long Island Rail Road had engineered trains to Plandome Village as early as 1913 when Manhasset's residents numbered only 1,000.

By 1951, however, Manhasset High School had been enlarged and the year before, the parishioners of St. Mary's Catholic Church had built a co-ed high school behind their elementary building. Shelter Rock Road was still a high-crowned, two-lane, death trap along which teenage boys drag-raced toward the white pillars of Consuelo Vanderbilt's old estate, and the site of the future Americana Shopping Center was just one long field from B. Altman's to Searingtown Road.

My parents – a first generation Irish-Catholic woman from Manhattan and a Confederate-familied, Presbyterian son of Texas, bought a three-bedroom, one-and-one-half bath Levitt house at 110 Mill Spring Road in North Strathmore for $34,000.

That was so many years ago and it seems like yesterday.

In fact, in the rosy vision of my mind's eye it looks as if everything went just one way then.

Ray, the Jablonski's bus driver, took the Strathmore children to school everyday, and Al, the policeman, made sure the walkers crossed Northern Boulevard safely. Echo picked up the trash.

The Gibsons and the Cardillos provided the newspapers, The Wright Brothers serviced hardware needs. The Ruggieros outfitted us for sports, filled our prescriptions and taxied us home.

The Jaffees hemmed our jeans without charge. Jimmy Brown, Manhasset's son, made football paradise of a fall Saturday at the high school.

The Grothiers hand-churned ice cream and served it in a gleaming clean parlor. Probably every teenager in town went to Town Hall Pharmacy or Jim and Joe's for a daily vanilla Coke, and the little children went to Sam Asher's in Munsey Park or up to Doc's Strathmore Drugs for the same.

The Gallaghers or Fairchilds buried us and the Andersons sent the flowers.

By 1952, even President Eisenhower had come to Manhasset (on the campaign trail), and soon Temple Judea and the Jehovah's Witness Hall joined houses of Quakers, Methodists, Baptists, Lutherans, Congregationalists, Episcopalians, Catholics, and one of the oldest of all, the Valley Church in Spinney Hill, where our family's friend Viney worshipped.

In my memory it was a Jimmy Stewart-Donna Reed kind of town. There was the North Shore Hospital fair, an annual soapbox derby for fathers and sons, a hula-hoop contest, and B. Altman's was host to block parties in the summer. On Halloween, their Charleston Gardens' Restaurant held costume luncheons for neighborhood children.

Santa Claus arrived at Arnold Constable's in a helicopter; he had his own log cabin outside Lord & Taylor's and a complete toyland trail through B. Altman's.

Many Manhasset girls took ballet lessons from Virginia Wheeler, and some young boys donned white gloves to take ballroom lessons at Fred Astaire Studios. We got working papers to be relish or popover girls at Lorraine Murphy's or her cousin, Pat's.

There were water ballets held at the country clubs and jazz nights at the Hotel James.

For the seedier-minded, there was the Strathmore Hotel, also known as The Scratch. Gary and the Wombats tuned up to appear at Gino's Restaurant, Bobby and the Orbits played at the proms, and men disembarked from the dry trains of the pre-bar-car railroad days.

Dugan's delivered fresh donuts to front doors in the mornings and Jonas, the milkman, actually left notes with his cream-topped bottles.

But the best part of Manhasset, the part that still lives in my dreams, was the open space of Chapel Woods.

The path began at the end of Albermarle Lane in Strathmore Vanderbilt. Through pine cozies and berry patches, my friends and I would walk, always ending in the same place: a sun-soaked field of wildflowers and grain, graced by an old oak tree.

We conquered time and space in the arms of that tree, and surely many others had before us, for there was an old, strong rope noosed about one of her upper branches. The rope hung at the crest of a grassy knoll, a sturdy foothold had been spliced into its end. With a good running start, we could pull the oak's branch back just far enough to fling ourselves out over the knoll. We'd soar, catching the wind and surfing on rays of the sun.

Once, recently, when I was at a loss for familiar things, I headed toward the end of Albermarle Lane with some slight hope that the oak might still be beyond the pine cozy somewhere.

But I stopped at Consuelo's gates and never passed on to Country Club Drive.

The view I have of that old tree is the only one I want.

- originally published in The New York Times, March 25, 1991.

Kindergarten

I clearly remember my first day of school.

As the youngest, before school age, I had routinely accompanied the rest of the family to the bus stop, the attendance office, or the classroom. So I was ready for kindergarten. I hungered for it. I longed to be a part of St. Mary's Elementary School.

First of all, everyone there was so nice.

The good Sisters of the Immaculate Heart of Mary patted my head and said I had "lovely manners" and repeatedly commented that I'd be a student before anyone could blink an eye. And they smelled wonderful, linen-fresh with an essence of talc. I even liked the way they sounded - how they clicked and rustled when they walked.

The entrance to the elementary school, up the Northern Boulevard stairs through two heavy oak doors, opened onto a yellow-lit, wainscoted vestibule and held my future.

The kindergarten room was to the left of the cavernous foyer, across from the principal's office, and separate from the long yellow and brown, first through fourth grade hallway that stretched between wide staircases leading to the upper grades.

Kindergarten was held in two sessions with more than 40 students per class. I was in the morning group, and I was delighted to be in a room so close to the Mother Superior's office.

Mother Annette had personally told my mother that the "little ones across the way were her favorites," and added that she loved how pretty all the little girls looked on the first day of school. She inspired me to be the prettiest.

Uniforms didn't come to St. Mary's until the late 50s, so shopping for back-to-school clothes before that was a family event.

"School bells ring and children sing: It's back to Robert Hall again."

Although we begged our parents to take us to this wonderful TV-land store, it never happened. We shopped at Best and Co. or B. Altman's; Arnold Constable's or Lord & Taylor's.

I used to long for a Robert Hall dress with a skirt that stood out like a toilet paper-doll-cover or a snow suit with a glow in the dark, zipper.

My mother didn't share my dreams.

I started my first day of school with a simple, plaid dress, white ankle socks from Best's and sensible Buster Brown shoes from the Manhasset Bootery.

I wasn't happy about my ensemble, but I did have a pencil case of my own choosing from the Nassau Stores and inside was a rocket-ship pencil sharpener that totally captivated me.

Not so for kindergarten teacher, Sister Mary Rosalie.

The Sister welcomed us and got into teaching right away. Her first lesson involved how to sit quietly with our hands folded on our desks, our knees together, and our feet flat on the floor.

Sister Rosalie believed the first order of all education was stillness, probably not a great method for five-year-olds.

I'm sure she meant well.

I saw Sister going around the room ordering fellow students "to store distracting objects" under the lids of their desks, so I hid my pencil sharpener in my pocket and tucked the case away as instructed.

I practiced hands-folded attention with the best of them: Johnnie and Paul. Bobby, Davey, Didi, and Danny. Lainy, Lynne and Mary Jo. Tish, Angie, Pam, and Kathie. Terry, Merrily, Linda, Ginger, and Mary Ann. Nancy, Patsy, Ruth, Peggy, and Carla. Jackie, Gus, and Tommy. Kevin, Billy, Larry, Timmy, Jimmie and Ralph; Jackie, Gregory, Joey, Tony, Brian, Stevie, Eddie, Sue Ellen, Barbara, Beth, Mickey, and Ricky.

Sister Rosalie cruised around the room, smiling and nodding her approval at our postures and our acquiescence.

Then she taught us how to stand - actually, she said how to "rise." With one lifting gesture of her two arms, we came to our feet in complete disorder. So we rose and sat to her command 20 more times until we did so in unison and relative silence. After rising, we learned "lining up" and "resting."

Resting involved a complicated positioning of our heads based on alternating rows, so that - at no time - were we ever tempted to break our stillness and engage the eyes of another.

While practicing this position interminably on a day of such excitement, the yellow and red rocket-ship began pulsating in my pocket.

With my hands folded below my head, and facing the assigned direction, I reached in and withdrew the forbidden, "distracting object."

I could hear Sister Rosalie's rosary beads brushing down the aisles behind my head. She spoke softly to a student who failed to keep his eyes closed. I squeezed my lids shut and curled my little hand around that pencil sharpener like it was my secret from the universe.

Confident that I was the boss of me, I must have relaxed my grip or twitched some liar-muscle known only to nuns because diminutive Sister Rosalie swooped on me and seized my distracting object with an "Ah-HA!" that rattled the entire class.

I hadn't known Sister's lesson plan intended to make an example of someone and I'd fallen into her trap.

She didn't pull me up to the front of the room, but she made a huge ordeal of smashing my rocket-ship pencil sharpener and throwing it in the trash.

I could feel everyone's fear.

Then Sister Rosalie performed the lifting gesture with her hands, and we all rose. She lowered her arms and we sat. She folded them and we rested.

I was in perfect repose, getting over the pencil sharpener incident, when Sister's finger softly touched my right shoulder.

"Miss McLain," Sister Rosalie said. "Mother Superior would like to have a word with you."

I have no idea what happened after that, but there was no more head-patting, I assure you. In fact, in my mind's ear what followed was a 12 year monologue about modeling my behavior after my older siblings if I ever wanted to amount to anything.

I'm not sure I took that advice, but I did learn one critical lesson from kindergarten.

Sister Rosalie taught me that I'll always be attracted to rocket ships and distracting objects - and - just because someone smells good, it doesn't mean she won't smash your new pencil sharpener.

Queen Mary

I have a photo of the girls in my first communion class in 1956. We are all 8 years old. It was May.

There were two communion classes each year, one for the kids who were eight years old at the beginning of second grade and the other for those who became eight after that.

The belief was that one reached the age of reason at the end of the seventh year of life, according to someone. Some pope, I guess, though I really never knew.

I had only enough sense to know it was not an age of reason for me, and that secret made me pretty nervous about committing myself to the whole affair. Reason-attainment meant you could take care of yourself and I didn't want to have to do that. I was high maintenance.

But I went along with First Communion because, like everyone else in my class, I was in love with our teacher, Sister Louisa.

She was about 22 and had twinkling eyes, Irish freckles and a very cute, giggling laugh.

She also smelled great. Like linen fresh from the line on a balmy day.

SUZANNE MCLAIN ROSENWASSER

Sister Louisa taught us all about how to "receive Communion" and what that meant.

I had a hard time on the meaning part because I got stuck on why anyone, the Son of God included, would want another "to eat His body and drink His blood."

However, I did learn the lesson about the capital "H," as you can see and I'd begun to write JMJ with a cross at the top of my papers. I just wasn't up for body eating.

The problem was, I knew all about cannibalism from the late night TV movies my brother let me watch when I couldn't sleep and he was babysitting. You know, the ones on "Shock-Theater" with that ghoulish host, Zacherly - ewwwww.

Nonetheless, though I didn't possess enough reason to distinguish between communion and zombies, I persisted with Sister Louisa's lessons and dealt with the weird nightmares since I also had another motivator. I was very fond of the First Communion dress my Aunt Mae was sewing for me. It was full length, white organza with puffed sleeves, covered buttons up the back and a satin sash. She made me a shoulder-length veil with hand-turned roses of satin ribbon at the crown.

Sister Louisa ooh-ed and ahhh-ed at my dress when she saw me the day of our big life passage. I was sure, oh so sure, that I would be chosen - as a girl from the second grade was each Spring - to crown the Blessed Virgin at a huge Queen of May ceremony held outdoors in which students from k-12 participated with families looking on.

After all my sister Mary, who was two classes ahead of me, had been chosen when she was in second grade and Aunt

Mae had made her dress, too. I had no doubt I was to be the one in 1956. I had the dress and the connections. I was in.

That must have been the first time I realized you can't dream yourself into a position of leadership when all you've got is a pretty dress.

My classmate, Sue Ellen, was named to crown the Blessed Virgin on May Day, and I resorted to little pageants at the May altar Mary and I built in our backyard with our mother's Virgin statue.

We made little buttercup and lily of the valley crowns and gathered "bowers of flowers."

We each had our own veil and didn't bother with our dresses. We'd take turns being the one who got to crown the Queen. I think we got confused with the wedding ceremony and threw petals before the designated crowner as she walked up a sheet toward the Virgin who was mounted on a rock, so she could be crowned from a ladder like they did at school.

We both sang the Queen of May song and processed, with the crowner climbing the ladder and placing the circle of wildflowers at the stressed word "NOW" when we sang: "We haste to-ooo crown thee-ee NOW."

Mary taught me how she was coached to place the crown on the Virgin's head and we did it just like that.

It seems like Mary and I played this game every spring for years. I know our veils were in tatters when our mother finally decided to throw them away.

A girl only gets one shot at crowning the May Queen, in case you didn't know. I'm glad Mary had it, and though she isn't alive to reminisce with anymore, she gave me the gift of this memory, and truly, it was always Mary who deserved to be the girl in our family who crowned the Virgin Queen in front of the whole school in a beautiful communion dress made just for her by our dear Aunt Mae.

The Recess Window and Nuns' Underwear

I graduated from the eighth grade of St. Mary's Elementary School in 1961. All those years, we climbed out a basement window in our cafeteria to get to the playground at recess.

I swear this is true.

Girls were instructed how to get out the window without flashing the entire lunch room, but trust me, the process was not conducive to maintaining a lady-like grace.

The wonder here is that no one objected - neither parents nor kids. When our turn came, we climbed two steps, sank to our knees, grabbed our skirts, and prayed we'd get out of there without a scene. Bumped heads and scraped backs were a normality.

Maybe we were just happy to get out of the clammy basement.

Actually there were two lunch rooms down there - in two-toned paint - glossy cream on top and battleship gray on bottom. Fluorescent lights cast a yellow pall over the long tables and the rickety benches that each sat five kids.

The main lunchroom had more windows than the one across the hall. The larger room was brighter because the kitchen staff needed to see what they were doing.

The small room was dark and only had six tables in front of the small set of stairs leading to the fire escape/recess departure window.

I'm sure someone reasoned we were killing two birds with one stone by practicing a disaster plan every day on our way to play.

There was a system to all of this.

We queued up in the main room according to the patterns set by our teachers who knew which of us would be unable to keep the silence required at lunch if we sat together.

We walked through the line sometimes asking Mrs. Madigan for mashed potatoes with gravy or maybe tomato soup with a grilled cheese sandwich and often a chocolate donut, but usually we brought our lunches in Davy Crockett or Dale Evans' boxes and only bought milk.

There were two or three nuns placed in the main lunch room, and they walked around holding their rosaries and praying silently as a tool to keep us quiet.

It worked, most of the time, because it is ingrained in pre-Vatican II Catholics to respect silence when in the presence of prayer.

The smaller room hardly held the tables and kids, much less the line of those crawling out the window, so only one sister was able to keep us in tow. To help when the Sister's prayers would not, the administration hung - high on each wall at either end of the room - concave, plaster images of

Jesus and Mary, the shape of which made their eyes follow our every move.

On good days the system ran like clockwork. Classes waited beyond the boiler room on the stairs until an entire group had exited the window to recess, thereby freeing up tables for incoming diners to occupy and allowing awaiting students to file into the cafeteria line.

But things didn't always go smoothly.

Sometimes a kid would forget his lunch money after he'd gotten a tray full of food, causing a monumental tie up, or two boys would start pushing each other until the whole line was swaying back and forth, or a kid would get a head wound bounding out the recess window too quickly.

Once, I rounded a corner too fast and bolted right into a nun while I was carrying a tray of tomato soup. Her entire blue habit took on the appearance of a blood bath. My friend thought this was very funny. While trying to apologize, I began to laugh. I was probably ten.

The nun was furious and spewed a litany of my sins at me: I was careless. I was always in a hurry to get nowhere. I had little regard for others, etc.

Then she turned to my giggling friend and told us to stand by the boiler room until lunch was over.

No recess for us.

When the last little butt exited the window to the playground, the offended Sister - now cleaned up - motioned for us to enter the small room and to stand in front of one of the benches. She stood at its other end and nodded when we were to be seated.

We knew the drill.

However, none of us calculated the fact that the two of us were on the far end of this rickety bench, so when we sat together the other end, at which Sister stood, flew up into the air and nearly struck her in the head.

My friend and I burst into hysteria when we hit the floor, only to open our eyes and see that this nun was closer to a rage of spoken impropriety than any we'd ever seen.

And I'd seen plenty of nuns in my time.

In fact, I considered myself a bit of a savant when it came to the genre. You see, my Aunt Fran - my mother's sister - was a Sister of Saint Dominic who taught in the Bronx.

When Aunt Fran visited our house, she was required to bring another sister if she was spending the night.

I saw them at bedtime; they wore little white caps that tied under their chins. I found this profoundly interesting and I tried to pick up whatever tips I could about nuns outside of school.

For instance, I learned that nuns drank.

Aunt Fran and friends enjoyed the 'milk shakes' my dad made with a wink which were just vanilla ice cream blended with gin, in moderation of course.

So this led to another thing I knew about nuns: They danced.

I loved it when my Aunt and her friends hiked their white, linen skirts up into their cinch belts and wound their long rosary beads around an arm to partake of an Irish jig in my parents' living room.

Moments like those made me think nuns were human, but I was convinced this was true when my friend showed me a catalogue from which her father sold goods to the convents in the New York area.

This was nun-porn as far as my 12 year old brain could figure. There were bras in that book and girdles and huge cotton panties and, no, could it be true? Oh my God wait until I reveal this: Nuns require sanitary belts and napkins.

I whispered these facts to every kid I knew, well, not the last part if it was a boy.

For some reason, harboring all this information prevented me from seeing eye-to-eye with so many of my teachers. I can't explain why except to say, I always thought it would have been so much easier on everyone if they'd just admitted they were human.

I went on to finish high school at St. Mary's, graduating in 1965.

Some of our class members entered religious orders and some of the sisters who taught us left the convent to pursue other dreams.

It was now post Vatican II, when everything we knew changed right before our eyes.

I went off to college in the fall of '65 wearing a raspberry heather outfit by Villager which included knee socks and Weejuns.

I came home for Thanksgiving in bell-bottomed, blue jeans and a fringed suede vest.

Aunt Fran visited us for the holiday showing off her knee-length habit and carrying a purse. We could even see her hair wisping out from a short veil. She was no longer required to bring a friend and asked for a whiskey straight up with water on the side.

I still had a long way to go before I matured enough to understand the strength and dedication it takes to define your beliefs, much less to act on them.

In many ways, the nuns and Vatican II taught me that.

There are times in life when the modern world forces us to start fresh and look at life anew, and that's a good thing - as long as we keep a small window open so we can climb out to play in the old world once in awhile.

Walking through the Fountains of Youth

The generation of Long Islanders born in the middle of the 20th century grew up walking.

There was a healthy bi-product to the practice, but no one really thought about it. We rode our bikes when we wanted to go some place quickly but, mostly, we walked - to a friend's house, to the grocery store, to choir practice, to school, to baby sit, to Miracle Mile, to mail a letter, to sell Girl Scout cookies, to play in a park in the spring or to ice skate on a pond in the winter, or to swim in the Bay come summer.

We had destinations we reached with a social interchange. When we walked alone, we were likely to meet up with others we knew who were walking somewhere, and we actually spoke with them and even walked with them for a while. We also walked in large groups of mixed genders or small groups of females only.

Even when we became licensed drivers we walked, since family cars were rarely available to drive. Consequently, Long Island kids of those decades knew our towns inside and out. We knew the short cuts and the street names; we knew the best places to sleigh ride and the least trafficked roads for an uninterrupted game of kickball, and we knew the location of every soda fountain within a five mile radius.

I walked the hamlet of Manhasset with my friends, trekking upon every boundary from Plandome Station to Manhasset Hills, up to Strathmore and down to Leeds' Pond. From all this walking, we knew our neighbors, our shopkeepers, as well as our civil servants, and they knew us, too.

The central focus of the social milagros was food; the place chosen had to have a soda fountain and, since we could only spend a dollar or less apiece, it had to be economical. The amazing thing is the options included at least 12 classic soda fountains along the sidewalks of Northern Boulevard from St. Mary's all the way up to J.J. Newberry's at the end of the Americana. Another five stood along Plandome Road, including the epitome of the family-owned, art-deco, soda fountain and ice cream parlor, Grothiers.

On walks home from school, up the Boulevard, we often stopped at Lamston's, the newer of the two Manhasset 5 and 10s. We roamed the aisles while waiting for lime-rickies to arrive at the counter. Other school days we walked to The Hayloft which served scorching hot and perfectly crisp, crinkle-cut, French fries with a side of homemade gravy.

For variety's sake, we walked to the Munsey Park Village Center where Sam Asher managed to squeeze a soda fountain into his cramped newspaper and tobacco store. A long wall of racked comic books bore a huge sign that read: "You touch, you buy." Mr. Asher guarded the staggered rows of candy bars from suspected thieves and called out our last names as a reminder that he knew where we lived. The only draw was Mr. Asher's creation of the perfect, fountain egg cream.

Across from B. Altman's, Strathmore Drugs was on a corner down from the Sunrise Market and The Little Brown Shoppe. It was a great place to refresh before spending hours walking along the Americana Shopping Center. Mike, the counter man, drew frothy Cokes from the fountain's spigot, plopping in a cherry on request.

Every week day most high-schoolers walked quickly to Ruggiero's Town Hall Pharmacy on Plandome Road at 3 p.m. The luncheonette became jammed with the overflow of teenagers milling around on the sidewalk by 3:10. In the 60s, The Ruggieros leased the fountain to a Greek man named George and his pretty wife, Jeannie. When the restaurant reached capacity, George locked the door and stood there with his arms crossed until a few kids finished eating. At the last morsel, George escorted them out the door, admitting their replacements.

In my youth, we walked the town among the villagers who helped raise us. I'd like to think our parents knew what they were doing when they refused to drive us places. Walking gave us a sense of purpose, and the soda fountains provided us with a sense of belonging.

These days we celebrate "International Walk to School Day" which asks us to slow down and walk. It seems that so many of the world's problems come down to oil, that walking and slowing down just might lead toward some solutions. We're walking to combat other issues, like breast cancer, and those efforts have created armies of peaceful strollers. Walking upright distinguished humans; it is essential to our species. Somehow along these paths, we become part of a procession that's moving forward step by step.

- originally appeared in **Long Island Woman**, *October 2010; awarded Long Island Press Association Best Magazine Feature, 2010.*

Santa Claus, St. Jane and St. Mary's: a Manhasset Christmas

Christmas in Manhasset began when Santa Claus landed in a helicopter behind Arnold Constable's at the corner of Shelter Rock Road and Northern Boulevard in the 1950s. It was a huge parking lot, extending all the way from Shelter Rock, behind Best & Co., W.J. Sloane and Gallagher's Funeral Home toward St. Mary's School and Anderson's Florist. Every year, the lot was packed with kids, their parents and the high school bands which rivaled each other, most politely, while blasting songs of the season.

There may have been balloons, but not much else other than the marked helicopter landing site, velvet-roped, brass poles, and a red carpet leading to the entrance of the store. When the jolly guy landed, he threw his sack on his back, burst forth with a few ho-ho-ho's and led the admiring crowd into the newly-decorated-for-Christmas store – a Winter Wonderland shoppers were seeing for the first time that season. I can still feel the rush of skipping, hand in hand with my father, toward a holiday store full of Ginny dolls, tri-pod easels and coonskin caps.

On the outskirts of Manhattan, the real Santa – who, as every New York kid knew, had already arrived in Herald Square after the Macy's parade – had to have some kind of dramatic surroundings to pull off his ruse in the 'burbs.

Lord & Taylor, never far from its fierce Fifth Avenue competitor, sat directly across the street from Arnold Constable's. At L&T's, Santa had his own outdoor, log cabin. It sat unoccupied all year with a sign on its door that told us Santa was busy in his North Pole workshop getting ready for Christmas.

But always, just before the arrival of the heli-ported Santa next door, and immediately following L&T's renowned daily routine of playing an employee-rousing National Anthem, little green elves began to dance around their log cabin. And, with the blast of a trumpet, Santa came out the side door of the white brick building, waving to the crowds who were walking to the Arnold Constable parking lot.

The L&T Santa went into his cabin which was all twinkly-lit, candy-cane studded, and open for lap business a full hour before the competition even landed. Some kids went to both Santas within the same two-hour period. My mother didn't know what to do with the lie when we begged her to go to see the other Santa, too, knowing she'd have to explain where all these Santas came from.

Apparently willing to believe anything, we accepted that they were 'helpers' and got on with it. The Santa at B. Altman's, who sat on a huge gold throne at the end of a Toyland Trail in the expansive store at The Gates, always seemed to be a more elegant reproduction of the original.

One year, he wore a pure, white velvet and snowy Ermine-furred suit. The trees that glittered behind his throne were also white that year, and the entire store looked like a fairy-blizzard had fallen gently over the counters and displays.

These Manhasset Christmas memories are a part of me, but the one that is the sharpest occurs in the old section of the church at St. Mary's on Northern Boulevard.

Our family rarely sat in the "new church," the back added to the other side of the altar in 1953. We preferred the dark oak, stucco-walled cocoon of the 350-seat original building. The choir loft and the old confessionals held comfort for us; our family sat just behind center and close to the left aisle.

Recapturing the image calls to mind many moments in that spot – my dad's hand in mine, playing slow-motion, thumb wars to keep me occupied during the Monsignor's sermons and my mother's car sermons about appropriate church behavior on the way home after Mass.

What I came to love about this spot in later years was my view of it from the choir loft, where I sang with about 40 other St. Mary's High School girls under the direction of Sister St. Jane, a young and vibrant member of the Immaculate Heart of Mary convent with the voice of an angel.

Sister St. Jane was a perfectionist who swept us into the music with the fervency of rapture. Conducting required her to tie her voluminous blue sleeves with elastic bands to prevent whipping the singers in the first row with flying serge.

When the director sang, her mouth created such a perfect 'o,' that little round dimples formed like amplifiers in her chin and the notes came out complete and full.

At Christmas, the choir came down from the loft, wearing white robes with red satin collars and carrying lighted candles, as we made our way up the aisles just after we'd sung the high canon of Christmas Eve Mass in Latin.

The solemnity of candlelight and the soft, familiar hymn of Bethlehem drew the focus of the congregants to the gathering of curly-haired girls processing toward the white marble altar where we assembled in perfectly practiced order and stood stock still.

Sister St. Jane, a master of her audience, took one porcelain white hand from the folds of her robe and held it, gently - like so - until every eye...every eye, was focused like a Buddhist on that point.

When her hand moved to the downbeat, we sang – one sound, 40 blended-voices, erupting into the hollows.

Young, sweet instruments swelled the church like the Monsignor's sermons never could; our notes swirled and rose to the pitch of the echoed "Fall on your knees! O hear the angel voices. O night Divine! O Night! O Holy Night when Christ was born."

Everyone loved us at that moment - everyone.

Sister St. Jane, Jesus, the living, the dead, the unborn. And we ourselves; oh, how we loved us then.

Jaffee's

I decided early on that I wasn't a babysitter. Listening to weird noises in strange houses where little sticky children slept was not worth the $.50 an hour I earned.

So in 1962, working papers in hand at 14, I landed a job at Sam and Al Jaffee's Department Store for twice my babysitting rate and then some: $1.05 an hour.

At first my duties included "learning the ropes," as Al Jaffee called it with the stub of an unlit cigar hanging from the corner of his mouth.

That meant understanding the system of shelves which surrounded the perimeter of the store and rose from the floor to the ceiling. The merchandise was accessed by ladders mounted on slick rails which we scooted to the location of the item a customer requested.

Stopping at, say, Lingerie/Female, we climbed up the rungs, reached for a flimsy cardboard box inscribed with a black crayon: ctn panties wht, size 22, and hoped all the other boxes of cotton panties didn't come down with it.

I worked with a St. Mary's friend, unless one of the Mr. Jaffees thought we were gabbing too much and threatened to schedule us on different days.

However, Sam Jaffee was a gruff man with a huge heart. His brother Al was just all heart - or maybe it was the other way around.

At any rate, my friend and I would get scolded for yapping while we stacked and restacked the endless piles of dungarees (that's what jeans were then), khakis, and Dickee's work pants that lined the three center aisles of the store.

Mr. Jaffee would say:

"That's it, you two. You're jawing all the time. That's it. No more working together."

But by the time he posted the schedule, he'd forgiven us because even he had to admit: we talked, but we worked all the while, and the store always looked neat and clean when we were on the floor.

Employment at Jaffee's was a great way to get to know any of the young men in town a girl might want to know, and from a very interesting perspective if said young men came into the store to buy pants.

One of the job skills acquired at Jaffee's was the correct way to prepare a pair of trousers for hemming, free of charge.

The customer emerged from the dressing room at the back - a square space with a curtain, nudged in next to the bathroom and the work room. As the young man stood facing a full length mirror, we pinched the fabric at the center of each rear pocket and snapped the pleat into the legs of the trousers, delicately of course, marking the hem line with chalk at the top of the shoe's heel.

Let's just say, this whole process was a wee bit awkward, but nonetheless, a great reason to discuss the inane with a boy who might otherwise never say a word to you.

We also learned how to fit shoes. There were four theater seats across a rear wall with an inventory from steel-tipped boots to PF Flyers behind it. The last task with which we were entrusted was the cash register.

It was a formidable opponent - a huge thing with keys that fought back when under pressure and little trays full of change which had to be tallied by hand to the penny without anything but one's math skills.

Uh-oh.

Mr. Jaffee taught us how to count forward when we gave change. After laying the bill across the tray and not in its slot, we were to count aloud, like so:

"Let's see, that was four, ninety-eight and two cents is five and five is ten."

Easy. Until the time I forgot and put a bill into the slot before I made change.

"There you go, Sir, and seven cents makes five. Thank you very much." The customer replied: "I gave you a ten." I looked down and fully understood for the first time why we were laying those bills horizontally while making change.

It was late in the day and too awkward to start counting out the register to see if the customer was not always right. So Mr. Jaffee gave the man, whom we'd never seen before, a five.

Later, when we counted out five dollars short, it came out of my little manila envelope of weekly pay.

At Jaffee's, we swept the floors, as well as the sidewalk, and cleaned the bathroom and showroom when customers weren't in the store. If we'd done that, we were to restack the men's pants or climb the ladders with newly marked boxes of underwear.

I worked at Jaffee's for two years, eventually earning $1.30 an hour with pay-for-performance raises.

It's only fair to add that a week after Mr. Jaffee dunned my pay for the five dollar discrepancy, he told me to pick out any Ship 'n' Shore blouse I wanted.

"You've worked hard this week, kiddo " he said in his sweetest gruff tone.

I came away with a lot from that old store, with its worn wooden floors and ancient dry goods' inventory.

Jaffee's was my introduction to ethics and responsibility in the work environment, with a lesson about how to effect change as well as how to make it.

The Original Americana

Kids who lived up by The Gates in North Strathmore in the early 1950s played in a field that stretched from B. Altman's to Searingtown Road.

We thought it belonged to us.

Little did we know that Frank Castagna, a young developer with great vision whose family company had owned the property since 1922, was thinking about that field as well.

While we were climbing trees or making trails through fresh blankets of snow, plans had been drawn for construction to take place on our field. It was the footprint for the foundation of the famed Americana Shopping Center, which today leases to Chanel, Tiffany, Prada, Fendi and friends.

In 2012 Castagna Realty, the parent company of the two most prestigious shopping and dining centers on Long Island (the Americana as well as Wheately Plaza in Greenvale), will celebrate its 90th anniversary.

Surely the Castagnas will look back on the Americana's humble beginnings when the rent was paid by "low-end" businesses while the company slowly crafted and funded Frank Castagna's end vision: Madison Avenue in suburbia.

These first stores were a paradise for Manhasset Baby Boomers who were ready to break free of Plandome Road and eager to head to places where the owners didn't know our names.

For years we'd been chased out of the Fifth Avenue department stores on Miracle Mile when it appeared to some staffer we were making the rounds trying on hats, squirting the perfumes, sampling the lipsticks and stretching out on the sofas in the Ladies' Lounge.

The new stores at the Americana were much more accommodating; in fact a few were down-right hospitable.

Businesses had begun to recognize the profit of marketing to kids who had pockets full of babysitting and lawn-mowing money to spend.

The first place that won our hearts was Lewis & Conger, a department store with areas that catered to kids. In the record department, 45s were half the price of the ones in the Manhasset Music Store and candy was sold in bulk from cases laden with chunks of white chocolate, trays of Nik-l-Nips, and strips of candy buttons. None of the pricey bonbons in paper cups that Altman's carried.

Welcome mats appeared all along the strip.

Leeds Drugs opened in 1961 with a soda fountain and luncheonette that offered tubs of dill pickles, free to anyone who sat and ordered something, even just a lime rickey.

The Charcoal Chef flipped juicy burgers at grills in the front window and served up baskets of fries with free refills when we ordered the special.

40

Down toward Searingtown Road, the August Moon Restaurant had a small, gift store that sold chewy, rice candies and mystifying, affordable Asian trinkets. I'd be remiss not to mention the Singapore Slings purchased when we got a bit older, though not old enough, legally.

One of the more enticing ad campaigns aimed at our teen wallets, however, came from Wise Shoes.

To pick up its winter business, the management installed a free jukebox of Top 40 hits and offered free bottles of Coke from a large cooler. A sign in the window invited kids to "Come in and dance in a pair of Wise shoes."

So we did.

We adopted the space as our personal American Bandstand, trying to get the boys who followed us up to the stores to come in and dance with us. According to my diary entries, our lures were unsuccessful.

The room was converted to a sales' space by the time Spring came. We didn't fret, though, because we had J.J. Newberry's - two floors and many square feet of perfect five-and-ten-cent store magic. A kid just couldn't get this stuff on Miracle Mile: fruity Tangee lipsticks, inappropriate gag gifts, a four-pose photo booth, and a vast audio department that sold portable record players and cheap guitars. Plus, Newberry's had a long, soda fountain where they served up fine, teen fare: Patty Cheese Melts with cheese fries. We frequented this store so often, a friend's dad started calling her "Newberry Sal."

Next to Newberry's, the huge, arched windows of Hills Foods looked out from a peak - its lights shining like a beacon above Northern Boulevard and Searingtown Road.

Hills was a super market when super was a modifier in the grocery business.

The size of the store alone was staggering to a family who had only shopped at Sunrise in The Gates, and occasionally Food Fair, both of which faded in comparison.

Hills was bright and cheerful. The produce and groceries were arranged in appetizing displays and the variety of choices, well, my mother never seemed to get over those.

Yes, The Americana offered limitless possibilities, and in many ways began the change that eventually took Manhasset from a small town to a large one.

Because, in addition to the world of chain stores, the Americana gave us "The Cinema Theater," a small fine arts' house which captured our attention when it showed Brigitte Bardot's "And Man Created Woman," much to the consternation of local priests, ministers, and parents.

After that, we made a point of stopping by to look over the posters, but I was out of college before I actually saw a film there. It was "Shaft" and it opened with a short called "Peaches." It was a night of revelations.

Through many years and a variety of steadily improving stores, The Americana morphed into Castagna's image, and eventually the face of Manhasset changed as well.

This was neither a good nor a bad thing. It was just progress.

When I go to The Americana today, I park behind the stores. There the sidewalks are familiar and the fence along the back of the lot helps frame the memory of Ralph in his tree house at the far end or of my brother smoking a stolen

Chesterfield over by the Village Bath Club or of my sister and me, running through a sunlit field with tall grass whipping at our shoulders.

Patricia Murphy:
A Candle Lit for Women and Popovers

I was a popover girl.

In today's world that term sounds like it should have a 1-900 number after it. But I was not that kind of popover girl. In fact there are hundreds of New York women of a certain age who were popover girls, too.

We're in Manhattan, Yonkers, Brooklyn, and Manhasset - with another contingent in Florida - all former sites of Patricia Murphy's Candlelight Inn Restaurants, where popovers - a light egg batter, baked into a crisp bubble - attracted diners from near and far.

Popovers were an important component in Murphy's success from the first day she opened her restaurant on Henry Street In Brooklyn Heights in 1930, despite the shadow of the Great Depression.

Miss Murphy offered her patrons a full lunch, one choice only, for 40-cents and two options at dinner: 65 or 85 cents. The meals included a limitless supply of popovers, dispensed by neighborhood girls dressed in gingham frocks who emerged from the kitchen with baskets of the steaming rolls until the last diners indicated they'd had enough.

According to Murphy's 1961, auto-biography **Glow of the Candlelight,** her initial investment of $60 eventually yielded a profit of $39 a day. The restaurateur mildly noted: "The popovers were a great success."

Murphy opened another Candlelight Inn on Madison Avenue at 60th Street in 1939.

She upgraded her menu, added more ovens to accommodate the demand for popovers and expanded into two adjacent buildings within a year.

Patricia Murphy was a single woman in her mid-30s who had conquered a male dominated industry in one of the restaurant capitals of the world.

The year Murphy became a millionaire, she was swept off her feet by a retired U.S. Navy Captain, James Eugene Kiernan. They were married in 1943.

Murphy and the Captain ran between the two restaurants, greeting customers whenever possible and always making sure suitable attire was worn by their patrons, even providing fresh cotton jackets for men in their shirtsleeves.

Captain Kiernan was convinced that a formal restaurant offering family dining was just what the developing suburbs of Long Island's North Shore needed and his wife, who had found the time to become an award-winning horticulturalist, concurred; but only if the spot included luxurious gardens and a greenhouse.

Patricia Murphy's Candlelight Inn, with gardens full of exotic flowers and blooming shrubs, appeared in Manhasset at the corner of Northern and Port Washington boulevards in 1949.

Murphy decorated her staff in the theme of the closest holiday and her tables with flora from her own gardens.

While waiting diners roamed her greenhouses, they enjoyed complimentary canapés, before ending up at the door to a gift shop which sold all sorts of Candlelight Inn brands from jams and breads to soaps and perfumes.

The new location was an overnight success. The gift shop alone grossed $40,000 its first year. Apparently, patrons were not only willing to wait up to an hour, but also to spend a few additional dollars, if it meant access to unlimited popovers.

In Manhasset, an entire kitchen below the main floor was devoted to popover production. It took 45 minutes for the batter to bubble and brown, so the baker had to be on his toes rotating the trays and managing enormous, cast-iron ovens.

As soon as a party was seated, someone asked for the popover girl and woe to the server who had to say she was in the kitchen awaiting the next batch. So popover girls ran up and down those stairs to meet the demand, an effort the servers rewarded with cash from their tips at the end of a shift.

As an aficionado and former distributor of Patricia Murphy's popovers let me affirm, those baked balloons could stand five inches tall and they were out-of-this-world delicious.

In fact once the pastry had been sufficiently dressed with butter, cottage cheese and jam, the first bite produced what we called "the popover effect." It was a kind of hum, a polite, vocal burst of epicurean satisfaction.

Patricia Murphy sold all three of her Candlelight Inn Restaurants in 1953, retaining co-ownership of the name, to open what she considered the perfect Candlelight in Yonkers the next year. From the start, she plated nearly 5,000 meals a day. Now a renowned restaurateur, Murphy still served moguls, first communion celebrants, popover girls, and her loyal Filipino kitchen staff with equal regard.

Her humble Newfoundland beginnings, as a clerk in her father's general store, had put her on a path that included attendance at one of Dwight Eisenhower's Inaugural Balls in 1957.

The same year Murphy's husband died suddenly. Nonetheless, she found the strength and opened the Bahia Mar Candlelight Inn at a Florida marina, once again drawing thousands to her tables, though less successfully in the long run.

Patricia Murphy Kiernan was laid to rest in Virginia's Arlington National Cemetery next to Captain Kiernan whose stone notes his service in two world wars. Patricia Murphy's grave marker merely records the dates of her life, 1905-1979. This seems an injustice to a woman who built an empire during a time when mostly men did such things.

So here is an appropriate epitaph:

"Patricia Murphy lit a candle for the occasions of our lives with a touch of beauty – and unlimited visits from the popover girl."

Patricia Murphy's Popovers

(from **Glow of Candlelight** by Patricia Murphy,
Prentice Hall: New York, 1961).

Preheat oven to 450 degrees.

Put 1/3 tsp. butter or Crisco in each muffin pan (or custard cup). Heat in hot (450) oven five minutes while making batter:

1/4 tsp. salt	2 eggs
1 c. sifted flour	1 TBL melted butter or Crisco
1 c. milk	

Sift flour and salt into a bowl. Beat eggs separately with rotary beater, then add milk and butter. Sift in flour, beating only long enough to make a smooth batter.

Fill hot muffin pans one-third each with batter. Bake at 450 for 30 minutes, then at 350 degrees for 15 minutes or until firm, brown, and popped. Keep oven door closed while baking. Makes six large popovers.

Pool Parties in the 60s

Nothing. Absolutely nothing was as much fun as the string of pool parties the North Shore country clubs held for teenagers during the summers of the early 60s.

Plandome, North Hempstead, The Village Bath Club, Strathmore. They all had parties and each was better than the one before.

It was the age that sat on the cusp of the Beatles and cut-off jeans, so the fact that the clubs required us to dress up for the events was not a problem. That's what we did. Many of us had taken ballroom lessons in white gloves and party shoes in these very same clubs. The lessons prepared us for the attire expected at such events. The boys wore shirts and ties and the girls, summer dresses with swirling skirts.

Our parents dropped us off at the entry to whatever club was hosting the evening's affair. We'd pay $2 to the Board members who stood at a gate and appraised us.

A gentleman was always positioned first to welcome each young guest with a handshake and a quick assessment, one that was repeated by every adult there. Another grown-up placed a literal stamp of approval upon each of us.

Chaperones routinely toured the party throngs to bounce the kids without stamped hands who had snuck in from the golf course and along the way, the adults would come upon couples standing together in the shadows.

"Back to the party, kids," they'd say, and we'd abide.

We brought our bathing suits, but I don't recall anyone ever going into the pool willingly, and if someone was caught pushing another clothed person in, there was a $25 fine.

None of these things were hindrances because there was always a major attraction: Bobby and the Orbits, a Huntington band that provided a soundtrack for an entire generation of kids on the North Shore and even had a hit record "Felicia" which sold 20,000 copies.

However the song that amped up the pool parties was the Orbits' cover of the Dovell's "You Can't Sit Down"." The band played it at least twice at every party and three times if we begged them long enough.

What's really remarkable is - and I have no reports from parents who supervised these events - I don't remember a whole lot of trouble or even drinking, for that matter. I'm sure it happened, and maybe my friends and I were still too "junior high" to be fully aware, but primarily my memories are of dancing under the stars in a pretty dress to a live band.

Blue pools shimmered with an eerie romantic glow under cool, starry skies. The Orbits sang:

"There's....a...moon out to-ni-i-ight. Uh. Uh. Uh. Oh, oh, oh my darlin'. There's a girl at my si-i-ide. Uh. Uh. Uh. Oh. Oh."

Boys would dance the girls over to dark areas by the locker rooms or places behind a trellis or a shadowed path that led to the tennis courts.

What happened then was "necking," a word adults spat from their mouths at us with dire warnings. However, having defied them, I can accurately report a fact I've concurred with others like me who spent time in those shadows:

Necking was accurately named because its area of fair play was clearly defined. Catholic kids, especially, needed that kind of clarity. It was the dividing line between venial sins - easy to commit - and mortal ones - not so much.

So the action at pool parties was mostly first base, and with a little luck a girl ended the night having kissed a guy who was a great dancer and who really got into it when the last song of the evening, The Isley Brothers' SHOUT! shook the windows of our parents' cars, in which they sat waiting to take us home.

The Triumvirate

Three Manhasset boys formed a group they called The Triumvirate in 1963.

They were young men who clearly studied Latin at St. Mary's because they had enacted Julius Caesar's plan to arrest the power from members of the teen aristocracy whom they considered to be hindrances to their success.

The Caesar of the group was a small, charismatic teen who loved music and was also a monumental flirt. He knew how to get a person's attention.

The Triumvirate printed up business cards and stationery bearing the group's name: THE TRIUMVIRATE and a stark triangle reading Caesar at the top and Pompey and Crassus at the other angles. "Veritas" the logo promised.

To spread their message, The Triumvirate used the media available to them: the telephone and the Town Hall Pharmacy soda fountain, gossip chain.

Caesar would call a few selected girls each night with messages from himself and his power brokers. The phone call would go like this:

"Is this Pat? Well, hello there. Tonight's your lucky night because this is Caesar calling from WNTY in Manhasset and we have a song going out to you from Pompey."

If indeed Pat was having a lucky night, she'd hear the needle of Caesar's record player put down on:

"Doo-doo de doobie doo. Doo-do de doobie doo. In the still-ill of the ni-ight.

Darlin' I held you, held you so ti-ight..."

On the other hand, if the girl had annoyed Pompey in some way, Caesar's call would go like this: "Well Pat, Pompey dedicated this song to you tonight, so listen closely."

Pompey's message would come out loud and clear: "I'm justa walkin' the dog. Let me show you how to walk the dog."

This type of put down would lead to the purpose of the engraved stationery and the gossip mill.

The Triumvirate began to post a weekly list on the wall outside Town Hall's soda fountain where public and private high school teens gathered at 3 p.m.

On their personalized, ecru stationery there appeared this title in bold type: OFFICIAL DOUCHE LIST.

I'm not sure the majority of The Triumvirate's public was entirely schooled in the term, however.

Nonetheless, Caesar et al, listed ten people who had offended them in some way - anyone from the most popular girl in their age group to one of their teachers.

Let me get this right out there: I reigned as number 1 on the list the last week it appeared.

The offense which earned me the top spot occurred when I had turned down Crassus after he asked me to his Junior Prom.

The back story was that Crassus had voted "No" on the Triumvirate's decision to list me.

He knew the reason for my refusal had to do with my mother thinking her Sophomore daughter was too young to go to a Junior Prom.

Everyone else knew this, too.

As a result, I don't recall sweating it too much. I may have even taken a vicarious thrill in being #1 on the list because I had the public on my side.

I took Latin, too, and understood what it meant to hold the support of the vox populi.

The day Caesar hung the list, a crowd gathered to read it and Crassus broke through. He reached up and crossed my name off.

It got real quiet.

Then Crassus pushed Caesar hard in the chest, Caesar pushed back, and the crowd called for blood.

That's when Mr. Ruggiero came outside and ripped the Douche List off the wall.

"You should all be ashamed of yourselves," he said directly to The Triumvirate and told them to go inside.

"The rest of you go home. The fountain's closed today. Go home and remember your manners before you come around here again."

Mr. Ruggiero called the boys' homes and put each of them on the phone to tell their mothers what they had done.

That was the end of The Triumvirate.

Caesar's mother grounded him from using the telephone, so that was the end of WNTY, too.

Potestas corrumpit, as the Romans and our Latin teacher would say. Potestas corrumpit.

Beach 9, Where Are You?

Whenever I find myself staring out over the salt water, my mind's eye plays a biopic.

Memories of childhood summers on Long Island in the 1950s come back to me, complete with the aromas, images and sounds.

I recall being a little girl on family journeys to Jones Beach, when trips often occurred spontaneously with the arrival of Uncle Edwin, who drove commercial vehicles in Manhattan.

At dawn on those summer days, he'd pack a Ford Woody with his wife, their brood, an aunt or two, some wooly Army blankets, a broken canvas umbrella and provisions to last until nightfall.

He'd pull into our driveway and wait for my parents to fill their Chevrolet Bel Air with three children, two red plaid Scotch coolers, a five-gallon spout thermos and two inflated Goodyear inner tubes.

Once on the road, my siblings and I would grip the backs of the front seat asking questions about time, as we joined the thousands of other families heading to the terminus of Wantagh State Parkway.

There are more than six miles of beachfront along the shores of Jones Beach State Park, which first opened to the public in 1929. We favored Beach 9 because it was the family beach, where the walk to the water was relatively short and there were no teenagers making out on neighboring towels.

Before being claimed by erosion in 1977, Beach 9 was sand castles and buried fathers; it was Mello-Roll ice cream cones and hot dogs so crisp they snapped when bitten.

Jones Beach State Park is still a veritable resort for the public that captures the adventures of summer. In its earlier years and mine, there was an outdoor wooden roller rink at the main boardwalk, and down on the point at Zach's Bay, the marine theater and Guy Lombardo presented musicals on a stage, floating over underground access tunnels for the actors. There were handball, deck tennis and shuffleboard courts; heated and diving pools; archery, golf, softball, fishing, rowing and nude bathing venues. The marvel is that Jones Beach continues to make it possible for a huge cross-section of people to never want to be anywhere else.

Our family stayed there all day, with the best trips ending when the dads and the children waded out to soft sandbars as our mothers sat on the shore. While we dashed to dig clams from little water spouts our fathers pointed at in the saturated sand, the women, with their hands shielding the sun, watched our silhouettes.

Later the grown-ups ate the raw clams with gulps of cold Rheingold beer, and the littlest children fell asleep swaddled in towels, each sun-kissed and golden, lying under night skies on the sand.

As a teenager, I made the same trip in a friend's Bonneville or Impala convertible with at least three other girls. We'd travel the Wantagh Parkway with the radio blaring and our long tresses streaming behind us, while we scream-sang Murray the K's summer "golden gassers." By this time, I'd graduated to West End 1, farther down the causeway. Here the beach pulsed with hundreds of like-tuned radios along a wide and lengthy swath of bleached sand.

This was where the parents weren't. It was where teens came from all over the island and the five boroughs of the city. At West End 1, a girl from Manhasset could fall in summer love with a boy from Whitestone.

There we heard stories of the next step in the Long Island beach hierarchy, Gilgo, which had a bar that sold alcohol. Later on, as college girls, we flirted on Gilgo beach for hours, drinking mai tais and watching surfers curl through waves out in the breakers.

During those summers we hit every shore we could find. We befriended guys with motorboats who took us water-skiing or racing over choppy water to Rye Playland in Westchester County. We lounged on Breezy Point, where the Irish family of a college roommate offered their weather-beaten house.

We met someone whose family owned a cabana at the old Atlantic Beach Club. On some nights, we drove to Half Moon Beach in Sands Point just to hear the Sound lap the sand, or we crashed in houses on Westhampton Beach after rubbing baby oil on ourselves all day and dancing at Morgan's White Cap most of the night.

In the years since, we — my husband, our children, our families and friends — have added Gardiner's, Peconic and Oyster bays, Sagaponack and Montauk to our list of beach trips.

And we were ready to visit more when we moved to Georgia — a landlocked suburb in Georgia.

And though we've known the beauty of beaches from coast to coast, we still long for those day trips, when we grabbed a towel and headed out to discover another beach along summery Long Island shores.

- originally appeared in **The New York Times**, *August, 2007.*

AFTERWORD

If you were a child of Manhasset in her early years, you probably know the names of the friends who inspired these stories.

You know them through a sibling or from babysitting or from ice-skating at Leeds or Copley ponds. Or maybe through scouting or Virginia Wheeler's dance classes or the soap box derby or the MHS Saturday afternoon football games.

We are the generations that knew Manhasset in her youth.

Our forefathers were from the boroughs of New York that housed them before William Levitt opened up the North Shore.

But many of us were born in Manhasset, at a small hospital called North Shore which sat up on a hill where it held wonderful country fairs to raise funds for its future.

We shared a screen-door-slapping childhood, roaming the streets in the safe womb of a world that knew who we were with just a few degrees of separation.

It was difficult to be anonymous in Manhasset.

All age groups from public and private schools merged on the ball fields, in the churches or the scouting programs.

The teens co-mingled at Jim and Joe's or Town Hall Pharmacy and the grown-ups made some of us take ballroom lessons at Country Clubs, where we mixed again at swim meets and pool parties.

The Manhasset kids who are Baby Boomers today know the local characters in JR Moehringer's TENDER BAR. They are our brothers, our class mates, our bartenders, our fellows who travelled the corridors of the same time period as we. They were altar boys, Little Leaguers, safety-patrol boys, wild boys, soldier boys as well as sprightly girls, confident girls, forever girls who still remember which one of the Gino's/Publicans' crowd they first kissed.

Those of us who have left Manhasset return to discover that Manhasset has never left us.

We carry a palpable sense of it.

We're drawn back together regardless of the years gone by. We find ourselves standing in a vaguely familiar place that's supposed to be Wright's Hardware and wish we could ring the door bells in the back one more time.

We drive to our former homes and find them somewhere in the shell of an upscaled renovation. We feel a small thrill when we spy old rock walls that still mark the lines between Munsey Park and Flower Hill.

We walk along the paths of what was once Memorial Field, closing our eyes to hear the crack of our brothers' bats and smell the honeysuckle around the tennis courts.

Within this collection of stories I included two **New York Times** features which have travelled back to me from Manhasset folks near and far, and another internet favorite "Walking to the Fountains of My Youth" which appeared in **Long Island Woman** and earned a Long Island Press Association Award.

I still share friendships with the "Manhasset kids" I've known all my life.

Without them I would have no stories.

Acknowledgements

So many of my childhood friends have made sure my Manhasset stories are told. Since the first story was published in the New York Times in 1991, my family and friends have passed them around - first by snail mail and then, in great profusions of emails to others who sent them on to their siblings and friends. To all, I am grateful. It is the circle of life in Manhasset and in the center of it, there is the essence of that wonderful old town we all knew so well.

There are specific folks who have always been there for my storytelling, so thanks to them:

My late sister, Mary McLain Smith, who shared these stories with me as long as she could, as well as her boys who've encouraged me along the way. My brother, Jim, who pointed the stories out in the newspaper to fellow LIRR travelers and his family for their "atta girl" support. Ginger "Ditta" Rickenbaker Hamby, who made me publish the "Beach 9" story. Leslie Phelan Droogan who worked as an unsolicited agent for passing the stories on whenever she had a chance. Lynne Muller McGrail and Tish McCarthy who are my personal memory banks for all things Manhasset. Also, thanks to Lainy

Duffy Grimm, Kathie Sansone Petrane and the late Terry Giesen Clear - the laughs and tears we've shared and shed are all over these pages. To Merrily Larkin who never forgot, Mary Grace Ruddy who found me after 48 years, and Kathleen Lombard Smyk who still calls.

To the Manhasset fathers I grew up with - a private thanks for being there when my own couldn't be, and to the all the boys I loved along the way to becoming a woman, well... thanks to those who love me still.

There are also a group of writing friends who brought me back to believing in what I do best: Helen Winslow Black who paid me great accolades on scribd.com; Ingrid Ricks, who featured my writing history on her blog; Barbara Alfaro who honored my words; and Laura Novak who never stopped encouraging me to send my work into cyberspace and beyond. We haven't met face to face, but we know each other heart to heart.

I have unending gratitude to my immediate family: My children Mia and Chris, as well as my son-in-law Chad, who always ask me to tell them stories and to my husband, Michael, who - more than any other person I've known or loved - is at the heart of all my tales.

~SMR

CPSIA information can be obtained at www.ICGtesting.com
Printed in the USA
LVOW110307070412

276576LV00005B/1/P